I Like to Be at Home

By Clem King

Some kids like to go on trips.

Bron and Jake hope to hike up a slope.

Some kids like to be at home.

Max rides his bike at home!

On a trip, you can swim in a cove.

Rose hopes to spot some fish in the cove!

At home, your mates can come and have fun.

If it is hot, you can run up to a hose!

On a trip, you can have a cone.

At home, Cole hangs a sack from a pole.

Cole can doze while he hangs.

Tate likes to go on trips!

His dad makes cake
on a camp stove.

I can bake in this stove at home!

The smell of cake hits my nose.
I like to be at home!

CHECKING FOR MEANING

1. What does Rose hope to see? *(Literal)*
2. What can you do at home when it is hot? *(Literal)*
3. Why would it feel nice to run past a hose when it is hot? *(Inferential)*

EXTENDING VOCABULARY

cove	What does the word *cove* mean? What is another word you could use instead of *cove*?
hose	Look at the word *hose*. What are the sounds in this word? What word can you make if you change the letter *h* to the letter *n*?
stove	The text has a camp stove and an indoor stove. What words can you use to describe a stove?

MOVING BEYOND THE TEXT

1. Do you prefer to go on trips or to be at home? Why?
2. Where might you like to go on a trip?
3. What are some things you can do at home that are difficult to do if you are on a trip?
4. What can you do on a trip when it is hot? What can you do when it is cold?

TIME TO WRITE

Write about what you like to do at home or about what you like to do on a holiday.

PRACTICE WORDS

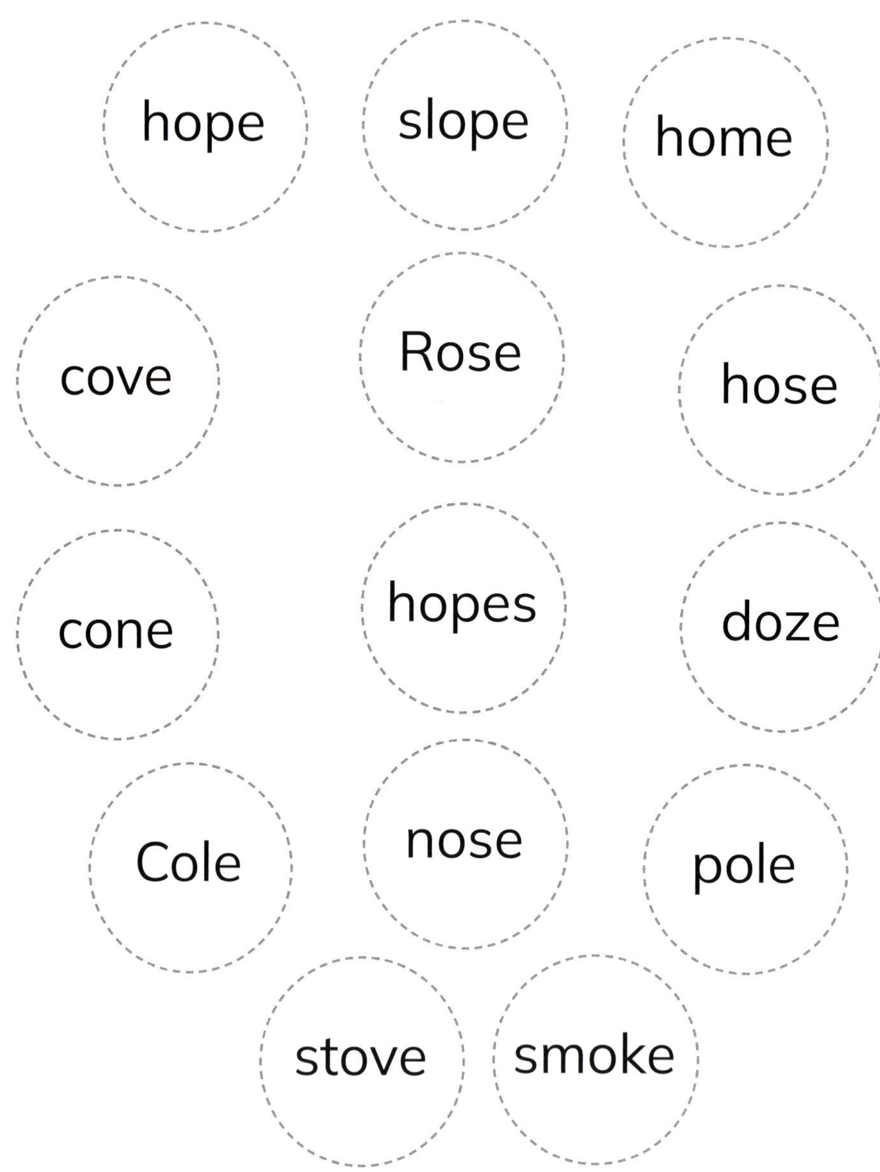